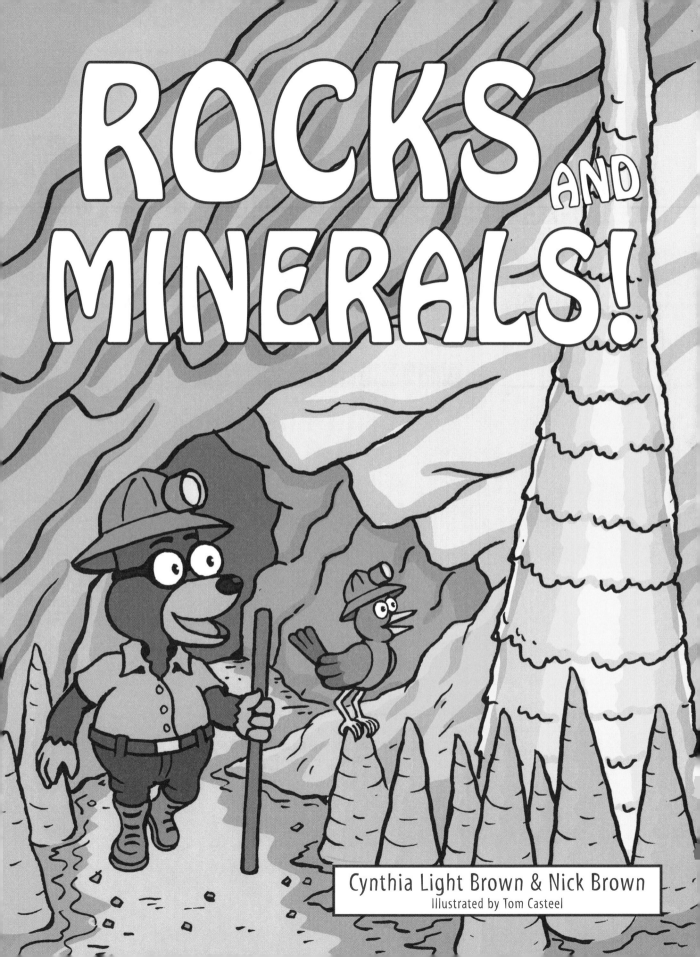

ROCKS AND MINERALS!

Cynthia Light Brown & Nick Brown

Illustrated by Tom Casteel

Titles in the **Explore Earth Science** Set

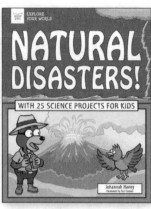

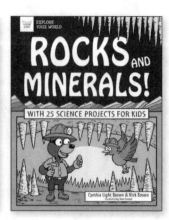

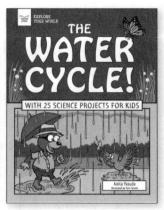

Check out more titles at www.nomadpress.net

Nomad Press

A division of Nomad Communications

10 9 8 7 6 5 4 3 2 1

This book was manufactured by Versa Press, East Peoria, Illinois
February 2020, Job #J19-11227
ISBN Softcover: 978-1-61930-874-9
ISBN Hardcover: 978-1-61930-871-8

Educational Consultant, Marla Conn

Questions regarding the ordering of this book should be addressed to
Nomad Press
2456 Christian St., White River Junction, VT 05001
www.nomadpress.net

Printed in the United States.

CONTENTS

Interested in primary sources? Look for this icon. Use a smartphone or tablet app to scan the QR code and explore more! Photos are also primary sources because a photograph takes a picture at the moment something happens.

You can find a list of URLs on the Resources page. If the QR code doesn't work, try searching the internet with the Keyword Prompts to find other helpful sources.

→ 🔎 EXPLORE ROCKS AND MINERALS

IGNEOUS ROCKS

About 95 percent of the top layer of the earth's crust is made of igneous rock.

SEDIMENTARY ROCKS

The sediment in sedimentary rock can include minerals, small pieces of plants, and other organic matter.

METAMORPHIC ROCKS

Metamorphic rocks are formed with heat and pressure as many millions of years pass by.

PUMICE

Many pumice rocks can float until they become too waterlogged and sink! Pumice is an igneous rock.

LIMESTONE

Most limestones form in clear, shallow, warm seawater. They are a sedimentary rock.

MARBLE

Marble is a metaphoric rock that often has gems such as rubies inside of it.

INTRODUCTION

ROCKS ARE EVERYWHERE!

Did you know that rocks and minerals are part of your life, every second of every minute of every day? Sound surprising? You stand on rocks, you consume rocks, and your home is built from rocks and powered by rocks. You even have rocks in the form of minerals inside you!

Those are some pretty good reasons to learn more about rocks and minerals. But the best reason of all is that rocks and minerals are fascinating. Rocks can slowly form during the course of millions and millions of years or be blasted from a volcano in an instant.

WORDS TO KNOW

rock: a solid, natural substance made up of minerals.

mineral: a naturally occurring solid found in rocks and in the ground. Rocks are made of minerals. Gold and diamonds are precious minerals.

1

Here are some places to find rocks and minerals.

✳ Electricity runs through copper and aluminum wires, which are made from minerals.

✳ Steel, made from the mineral iron, is used in the construction of buildings and vehicles.

✳ Houses contain nails, bricks, and plaster, which all come from rocks.

✳ Salt for seasoning food is a mineral.

✳ Plants grow in soil, which forms from rocks.

✳ Your bones are made mostly of a mineral called apatite.

✳ The earth itself is one big ball of rocks!

SCIENTISTS STUDY ROCKS FROM MOUNTAIN PEAKS TO UNDERSTAND THE HISTORY OF THE EARTH.

Rocks are like puzzles that can tell us about the earth's history. Right where you're standing, there might have once been an ocean. Maybe there was a volcano or even a huge mountain chain as big as the Himalayas. The rocks found below your feet can give you clues about the past.

THE BIGGEST ROCK OF ALL

Himalayas: a mountain chain between India and Tibet. It contains the world's highest mountain, Mount Everest, which is 29,029 feet above sea level.

crust: the thin, outer layer of the earth.

mantle: the middle layer of the earth between the crust and the core.

core: the center of the earth, composed of the metals iron and nickel. The core has a solid inner core and a liquid outer core.

WORDS ⊙ KNOW

You don't have to go far to study a really big rock. Just look down! The planet we live on is a really large rock made up of lots of smaller rocks. Let's take a look at the structure of the earth.

No one has traveled to the center of the earth, but we know some things about what's inside. We know that the planet is made of layers that have different kinds of rocks. The three major layers are the crust on the outside, the mantle in the middle, and the core at the center.

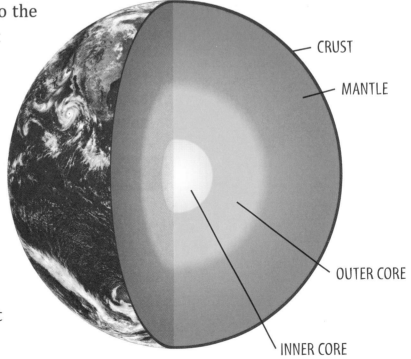

CRUST

MANTLE

OUTER CORE

INNER CORE

These layers probably formed as the earth itself was forming. We know that it gets hotter toward the center and there is a lot more **pressure** there. This makes sense, because there is always more pressure when there is more force pushing on something.

If you lie down on the floor and two friends lie on top of you, you will feel pressure from their weight. You might also feel hotter after a while, because pressure makes temperatures increase. The same is true for rocks closer to the center of the earth. They feel a LOT more pressure because of the weight of the rocks on them. They also have higher temperatures!

If you could travel to the center of the earth, what would you see? Let's take a look!

⋯ DID YOU KNOW? ⋯⋯

Ask an adult to hard boil an egg. Break the egg open. The shell of the egg compared to the whole egg is about as thick as the crust is to the whole earth. The white of the egg is like the mantle and the yellow yolk is like the earth's core.

START AT THE CRUST

On your imaginary trip, you would start at the crust, which is the thin, hard, outer layer of the earth. If you were standing on a **continent**, you would have to tunnel through crust anywhere from 16 to 56 miles thick. That may sound like a lot, but it's really not very much compared to the rest of the earth.

The rocks in the crust would look a lot like those on the surface. However, you might feel a bit warm, because they're about twice as hot as boiling water.

WORDS TO KNOW

magma: hot, partially melted rock below the surface of the earth.

lava: magma that has risen to the surface of the earth.

MANTLE IN THE MIDDLE

At the base of the crust, things would start to change. Better make sure you have some heat protection! The mantle is much hotter than the crust—about 1,000 degrees Fahrenheit (1,600 degrees Celsius) or more. It's about 1,800 miles thick.

The rocks would be darker and heavier. They would also be softer, because it's so hot. Mantle rocks are a bit like Silly Putty, which gets softer if you squeeze it in your warm hands. The rocks are soft enough that they move around very slowly. In parts of the mantle, especially in the very upper mantle near the crust, the rocks are partly melted and move around more. The melted parts are called magma.

SOMETIMES, MAGMA ESCAPES FROM UNDER THE CRUST. THEN, IT'S CALLED lava. THAT'S WHAT CAN FLOW OUT OF VOLCANOES!

5

THE CORE OF THE MATTER

If you keep going, you'll come to the core of the earth. The outer core is so hot that it's liquid. The inner core is solid. All of the core is made of metal, mostly iron and some nickel. The core is the thickest layer of all—about 2,100 miles thick.

The inner core is about 7,000 degrees Fahrenheit (4,000 degrees Celsius). It might be even hotter. That's 20 times hotter than your oven when you bake cookies and almost as hot as the surface of the sun!

DID YOU KNOW?

If you traveled to the center of the earth in a car going 55 miles per hour, here is how long it would take to go through the layers.

Crust: almost 1 hour
Mantle: 32 more hours, or 33 hours total
Core: 40 more hours, or 73 hours total

How can the inner core be solid? Don't things melt when they get hotter? They do, but the inner core also has lots of pressure on all sides from the weight of the earth. That much pressure keeps the inner core rocks from flowing. They're locked in place!

Keep the enormous rock of the earth in mind as we learn more about the smaller rocks that can be found all around us! In this book, you'll learn all about minerals, such as salt, gold, and iron. You'll discover the different types of rocks and how they form. You'll also learn more about the forces at work on our home planet, Earth. Then, explore all of these ideas with fun projects and activities.

Rocks and minerals are all around you, and each one has a story to tell. Get ready to rock and learn!

HOW DO WE KNOW ABOUT THE INSIDE OF THE EARTH?

No one has ever been to the center of the earth. Even just a few miles beneath the surface, the pressure is too great for humans to survive. The deepest hole ever drilled was in 1989 in Russia. It tunnels 7 miles below the surface—not even close to the bottom of the crust. So, how do **geologists** know what the inside of the earth is like?

* **Earthquakes** happen when **tectonic plates** in the earth's crust slip along a **fault**. An earthquake makes the ground vibrate in all directions. These vibrations are called **seismic waves**. Seismic waves can travel faster or slower and can change direction, depending on what kind of material they're traveling through. Geologists measure how long it takes these waves to travel through parts of the earth. Then, they can figure out what some of the materials below the surface of the earth are and where rocks are liquid or solid.

* There are some volcanic eruptions that bring up chunks from the mantle as deep as 93 miles.

* Scientists run tests in the laboratory using very high temperatures and pressures similar to those deep in the earth.

* Scientists think that the earth was formed from the same material as **meteorites**, so they analyze meteorites when they fall to the earth.

geologist: a scientist who studies geology, which is the history and structure of the earth and its rocks.

earthquake: a sudden movement of the earth's crust caused by tectonic plates slipping along a fault.

tectonic plates: large sections of the earth's crust that move on top of the hot, melted layer below.

fault: a crack in the earth's crust where tectonic plates move against each other.

seismic wave: the wave of energy that travels outward from an earthquake.

meteorite: a meteoroid that is not burned up by the earth's atmosphere, so it hits the earth's surface. A meteoroid is a rock that orbits the sun. It is smaller than an asteroid and at least as large as a speck of dust.

WORDS to KNOW

(PS) One way we learn about what's under the surface of the earth is by studying seismic waves. **Take a look at how scientists discovered the inner and outer cores!**

🔍 SCIENCE CHANNEL CORE EARTH

GOOD SCIENCE PRACTICES

Every good scientist keeps a science journal! Choose a notebook to use as your science journal. Write down your ideas, observations, and comparisons as you read this book.

For each project in this book, make and use a scientific method worksheet, like the one shown here. Scientists use the scientific method to keep their experiments organized. A scientific method worksheet will help you keep track of your observations and results.

Each chapter of this book begins with a question to help guide your exploration of rocks and minerals.

Scientific Method Worksheet

Question: What are we trying to find out? What problem are we trying to solve?

Research: What information is already known?

Hypothesis/Prediction: What do I think the answer will be?

Equipment: What supplies do I need?

Method: What steps will I follow?

Results: What happened? Why?

? INVESTIGATE!

Where can you find some rocks and minerals to study?

Keep the question in your mind as you read the chapter. Record your thoughts, questions, and observations in your science journal. At the end of each chapter, use your science journal to record your thoughts and answers. Does your answer change as you read the chapter?

MAKE YOUR OWN EARTH

Create a yummy treat that shows off the layers of the earth with every bite.

Caution: Ask an adult to help with the knife and melting the chocolate.

1 Mix the peanut butter and sugar together in the mixing bowl. Add flour until it forms a soft but firm dough. Form the dough into balls about 1 inch across. Chill in the fridge for a short time.

2 Cut the balls in half and scoop out the center of each half. Using the knife, fill the holes with jam, and place a chocolate chip in one half of each of the balls. Then, put the two halves back together.

3 With an adult's help, melt the remaining chocolate chips in the microwave. Remove the bowl from the microwave using potholders. Roll the balls in the chocolate and place them on the wax paper—be careful, the chocolate is HOT!

4 Roll the balls in the coconut. Cut one open to look at your layers, and . . . yum! Who knew the earth could taste so good?

SUPPLIES

* mixing bowl and spoon
* 1 cup peanut butter
* 1 cup sugar
* flour, as needed
* butter knife
* jam
* ½ cup chocolate chips
* microwave-safe bowl
* microwave oven
* potholders
* wax paper
* shredded coconut

THINK ABOUT IT: The earth is composed of layers. Here's what your concoction represents:

Chocolate chip = Inner, solid core

Jam = Outer, liquid core

Peanut Butter Mixture = Mantle

Outer Chocolate Layer = Crust

Coconut = Soil and plants

CHAPTER 1

POWERFUL TECTONIC PLATES

Planet Earth. You touch it every day. You've spent your entire life on it. It's your home. We all live on a giant ball called Earth. But we see only what's on the very outside of it. The inside is quite different. Even the crust of the earth where we live behaves in ways that you might not imagine!

The ground beneath your feet might seem solid, quiet, and unchanging. But things aren't always what they seem! In fact, the earth is always changing and moving, even if it's usually too slowly for us to notice.

? **INVESTIGATE!**

How does movement on the surface and deep inside the earth create new rocks?

The earth's crust, along with the very upper part of the mantle, is actually made of several enormous pieces of crust called tectonic plates. Around the planet, 12 huge plates and some smaller plates fit together like a jigsaw puzzle. They constantly move around—a bit like solid rafts floating on the gooey mantle below them.

These plates move apart and bump against each other, producing earthquakes and volcanoes and building mountains. This is called plate tectonics.

volcano: an opening in the earth's surface through which lava, ash, and gases can burst out.

plate tectonics: the theory that describes how tectonic plates in the earth's crust move slowly and interact with each other to produce earthquakes, volcanoes, and mountains.

recycle: to use something again.

WORDS ᴛᴏ KNOW

DID YOU KNOW?

Most of the earth's tectonic plates move about ½ to 1 inch per year. The plate beneath Australia is a speed demon, though. It's moving north more than 6 inches each year!

THE EARTH IS A GIANT RECYCLING MACHINE!

Earth has been recycling crust for a very long time—long before humans ever thought of recycling. New crust forms where tectonic plates move apart and magma rises to the surface. Think of the crust as a rigid board. As two plates move apart, the other end of each plate collides with other crust. When they collide, one plate is pushed under and melts. Crust is created on one end and destroyed on the other. Eventually, that melted crust moves through the mantle and becomes part of new crust.

erosion: the process of wearing down the earth's surface, usually by water, wind, or ice.

boundary: a line that marks a limit of an area.

divergent boundary: where two tectonic plates are moving in opposite directions and pulling apart, creating a rift zone. New crust forms at rift zones from the magma pushing through the crust.

rift: an area where the earth's crust is being pulled apart.

WORDS ⓉⓄ KNOW

ON THE EDGE

Erosion, earthquakes, volcanoes, and mountains are all the result of the movement of the earth's tectonic plates. Most of the action happens at plate boundaries, where one tectonic plate meets another. There are three different kinds of plate boundaries. Let's take a look at each of them.

Divergent boundary: This is where plates pull apart. Hot magma rises from the mantle. When it reaches the crust, it causes the plates above it to move apart, or rift. The rising magma pushes out through the openings, then cools and hardens to form new rocks. New crust is being made!

Nearly all the earth's new crust forms at divergent boundaries. Most of these are under the ocean.

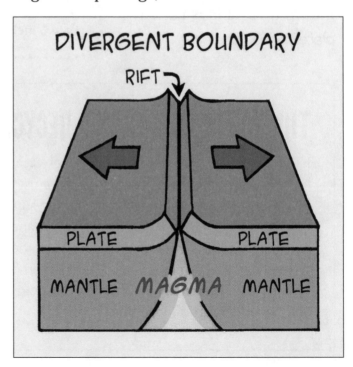

DIVERGENT BOUNDARY

RIFT

PLATE   PLATE

MANTLE *MAGMA* MANTLE

convergent boundary: where two tectonic plates move toward each other and come together, forming mountains and volcanoes and causing earthquakes.

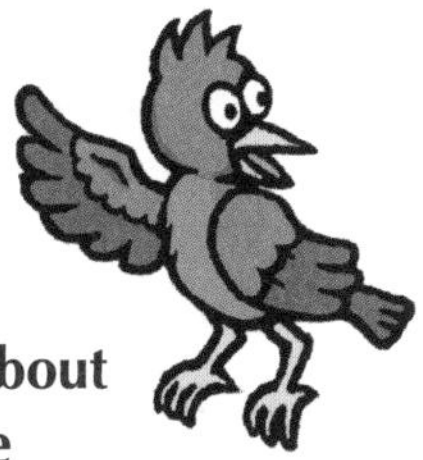

oceanic crust: the earth's crust under the oceans.

dense: tightly packed.

continental crust: the part of the earth's crust that forms the continents.

WORDS ⊙ KNOW

Convergent boundary: This is where tectonic plates smash together. What happens when two plates bump up against each other? That depends on the kind of crust the plates are made of. Oceanic crust, or crust under the ocean, is denser and thinner than continental crust, which is crust under the land we walk on.

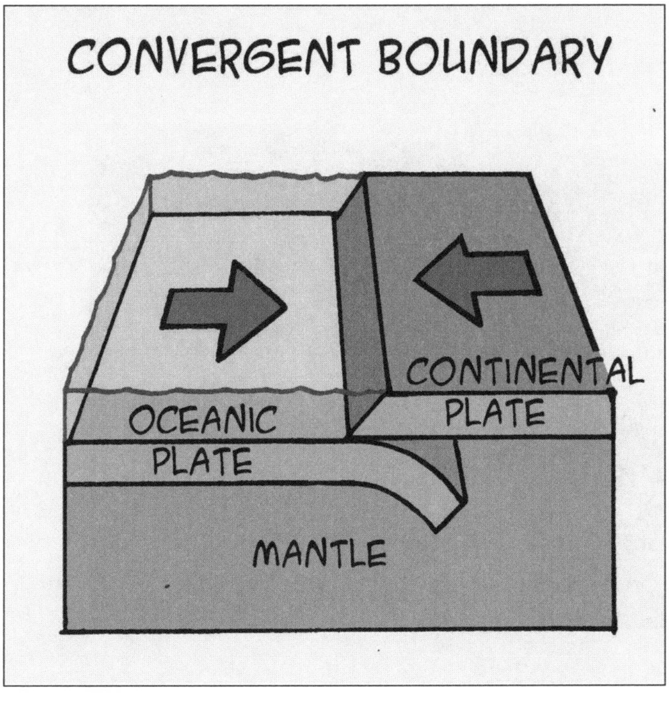

CONVERGENT BOUNDARY

OCEANIC PLATE

CONTINENTAL PLATE

MANTLE

When an oceanic plate and a continental plate collide, the oceanic plate slides underneath the continental plate because it is denser. Volcanoes often erupt around these boundaries. If continental crust collides with continental crust, they both buckle upward, forming mountains.

Transform boundary: This is where tectonic plates move past each other. Sometimes, plates grind against each other as they move side by side. As the plates move, they sometimes suddenly slip. This results in the release of a huge amount of energy and a lot of motion. That motion is an earthquake! California has earthquakes because it is sitting on plates that move past each other.

How do we know so much about what's going on under the surface of the earth? It took a while to learn!

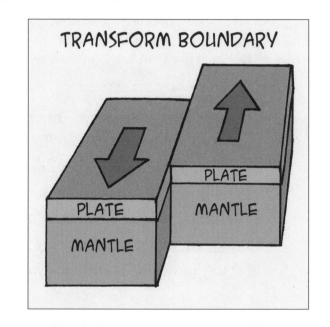

TRANSFORM BOUNDARY

PLATE

MANTLE

PLATE

MANTLE

A RIFT MADE BY TWO TECTONIC PLATES IN ICELAND

BIRTH OF AN IDEA

Alfred Lothar Wegener (1880–1930), a German explorer who also studied astronomy, first developed the theory of continental drift. He believed that all the continents had been joined together at one time long ago.

Wegener didn't know how or why the continents had drifted apart, but he saw how the continents might fit together. When he made a speech about his theories in 1923, though, some other geologists thought he was very wrong.

theory: an unproven idea that tries to explain why something is the way it is.

continental drift: the theory that explains how the continents have shifted on the earth's surface.

WORDS ⊚ KNOW

DID YOU KNOW?

At 29,029 feet, Mount Everest in the Himalayas is the highest point above sea level on Earth. Mount Everest exists because two continental plates are pushing together. And the mountain is still rising about one centimeter every year because the plates are still slamming together!

WHAT'S IN OUR BASEMENT?

Very old rocks! The earth's continental crust has a basement, just as many houses do. The continents have very old rocks at their center. Geologists call them "basement rocks." In most places, these old rocks are covered with younger rocks, but in some places, they're exposed on the surface. The oldest rock found is more than 4 billion years old! The crust under the oceans is about 20 times younger—less than 200 million years old. Oceanic crust keeps getting recycled because of plate tectonics.

Then, in 1960, Harry Hess (1906–1969) suggested that ocean floors aren't permanent. He said that the ocean floors are spreading out from the middle. At their edges, where they meet continental crust, the oceanic crust is dragged down into the mantle below. This would also cause the continents to move.

WHAT DID THE TECTONIC PLATE SAY AFTER AN EARTHQUAKE?

It wasn't my fault!

At first, other geologists didn't agree with these ideas. But then, they found some evidence under the ocean. Ridges of raised rock run down the centers of the oceans. Scientists found that on both sides of the ridges, rocks are older the farther away from the ridges they are. Other scientists gathered more evidence to support the theory of plate tectonics. It took more than half a century, but Alfred Wegener was finally proved right!

Learn more about Alfred Wegener and his work in this animated video.

🔍 ALFRED WEGENER VIDEO

Now that we've learned about tectonic plates, let's take a look at something smaller in the next chapter—minerals and crystals!

? CONSIDER AND DISCUSS

It's time to consider and discuss: How does movement on the surface and deep inside the earth create new rocks?

PROJECT!

CHECK OUT OCEAN RIDGES

You can use Google Earth to look at a ridge in the Atlantic Ocean that forms a plate boundary.

> **Get an adult's permission before using the internet.**

1 Go to Google Earth. — — →

2 On the left, click the icon of a magnifying glass (search) and type "Mid-Atlantic Ridge."

3 Click the minus sign (–) in the lower right to zoom out. Zoom out far enough to see the whole Atlantic Ocean. Do you see vertical lines? Those are where the oceanic crust is rifting apart.

TRY THIS! Click a spot and drag to look at a different place. Can you find other features of plate tectonics?

BATTLE OF THE BULGE

Mount Everest is the highest mountain in the world, but it's not the point farthest from the center of the earth! Because of its spinning, the earth bulges outward a bit (about 26 miles) at the **equator** compared with the North and South Poles. Chimborazo Peak in Ecuador is only 7,113 feet above sea level, but it's the farthest point from the center of the earth because it's located close to the bulging equator.

WORDS TO KNOW

Mid-Atlantic Ridge: a plate boundary on the floor of the Atlantic Ocean, and part of the longest mountain range in the world.

equator: the imaginary line around the earth halfway between the North and South Poles.

17

PROJECT!

SWEET PLATE BOUNDARIES

SUPPLIES

* candy bar with layers such as a Milky Way
* solid chocolate candy bar
* table knife (one that isn't sharp)

Scientists use models to better understand the topics they're studying. You can model plate tectonics in a very sweet way!

Caution: Have an adult help with the knife.

1 Cut one end from the layered candy bar—just enough to see inside. How is the candy bar like the earth? How are the layers like the layers in the earth? How are they different?

2 Using the knife, make a crack in the chocolate across the top middle part of the layered candy bar. This is like a divergent boundary and the chocolate on each side of the crack represents different plates in the crust.

3 Grab the candy bar on each end and slowly pull apart, about 1 inch or less. This is like the plates in a divergent boundary moving apart. What does the gooey layer underneath do? This represents the mantle, which is soft and stretchy.

4 Push the layers back together, then push one side forward and pull the other side back. Is this hard to do? This represents what happens at a transform boundary, where the plates move past each other.

5 Take half the layered candy bar in one hand and the solid chocolate bar in the other hand. Push the two candy bars together, letting the solid chocolate bar go underneath the layered bar. This represents a convergent boundary where the plates smash together. The solid chocolate bar is oceanic crust, which is thinner and denser, and the layered bar is continental crust, which is thicker. Which crust will go on top and which will go on the bottom?

THINK ABOUT IT: The earth is composed of layers. A Milky Way has a top chocolate layer that is like the earth's crust. The fluffy layer underneath is like the mantle. When you pull apart the ends of the candy bar, it is similar to plates pulling apart at a boundary. During real rifting, though, the gooey mantle layer would well up with magma **erupting** at the surface. Which kind of plate boundary do you think might cause earthquakes?

WORDS TO KNOW

erupt: to burst out suddenly, such as in a volcano.

PROJECT!

THE DEEPER YOU GO

SUPPLIES

* empty large plastic milk or soda bottle
* thumbtack
* ruler
* a tray at least 2 feet wide
* water

Have you ever gone swimming deep underwater? Did you feel pressure on your ears? As you go deeper in the earth, pressure increases—a lot! Try this experiment to see how depth increases water pressure.

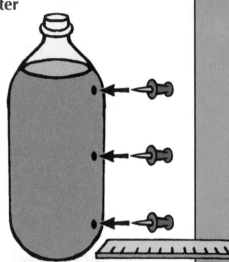

1 Use the thumbtack to make a hole near the bottom of the bottle, just above the bottom curve of the bottle.

2 Make a second hole near the top of the bottle, below the upper curve of the bottle and on the same side as the first hole. Make a third hole in the middle.

3 What do you think will happen when you fill the bottle with water? Write down your prediction in your science journal. Place the bottle on the tray, or outside, to catch the water.

4 Fill the bottle with water. What happens? Measure how far each hole is from the top and the horizontal distance that the water travels from each hole. Record your findings.

THINK ABOUT IT: Why do you think there are differences in how far the water travels from each hole? What happens if you turn up the pressure on a hose—does the water squirt farther? What does this suggest about pressure deep in the earth?

CHOCOLATE RIFT ZONE

Try this activity to model how magma pushes up through crust that's pulling apart.

Caution: Have an adult help with the stove.

1 Put the chocolate in the saucepan. Melt it over low heat.

2 Pour the chocolate into the baking pan. **Be careful, the chocolate is HOT!**

3 Let the chocolate cool slightly. Set two graham crackers next to each other on top of the chocolate. Slowly push them apart and slightly down. What happens to the chocolate?

···· **DID YOU KNOW?** ·····

Several times in the past, all of the land on Earth came together into one huge supercontinent, then slowly broke apart into smaller continents. The last supercontinent was called Pangaea. It broke into the continents we know today about 175 million years ago.

THINK ABOUT IT: The graham crackers represent the crust, and the chocolate represents the melted magma from the mantle underneath. As the crust separates, the magma gets pushed to the top.

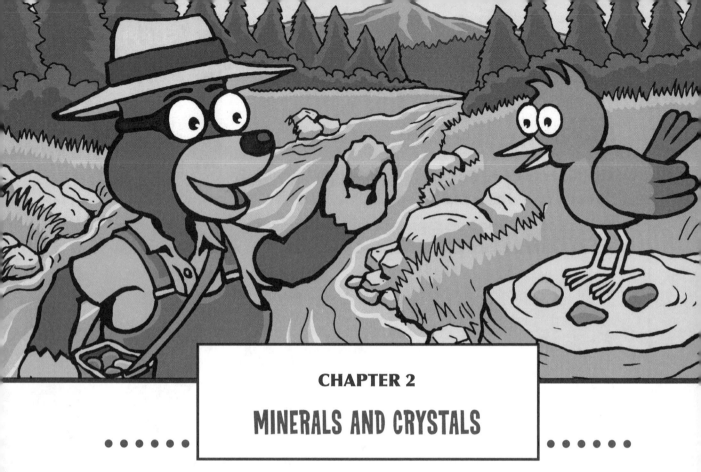

CHAPTER 2

MINERALS AND CRYSTALS

Have you ever picked up a rock and seen little specks
sparkling in the sunlight? You were probably seeing
minerals. Minerals can be so small you can't see them,
or they can be as big as a tree trunk. They can be
almost any color you can imagine. Minerals are solid,
natural substances that all rocks are made of.

Almost all minerals form as crystals. If you pick up a round,
smooth pebble, you might not believe that minerals are made of
crystals. Crystals have edges, right? True, but even pebbles are
made of crystals. The crystals are
just too small for you to see. Or,
maybe the pebble bounced around
in a river, which smoothed over the
rough edges of the crystals.

? INVESTIGATE!

What makes one type
of mineral different
from another?

To understand rocks, you must know about the kinds of atoms that make up minerals. You must also understand how those atoms are arranged.

ATOMS

Everything in the universe—you, the air, the sun—is made up of tiny particles called atoms, including rocks and minerals. In nature, there are 94 kinds of atoms, and everything in the universe is made of some combination of these atoms.

crystal: a solid with atoms arranged in a geometric pattern.

atom: a very small piece of matter. Atoms are the tiny building blocks of everything in the universe.

universe: everything that exists, everywhere.

geometric: straight lines or simple shapes such as triangles or squares.

carbon: the building block of most living things, including plants, as well as diamonds, charcoal, and graphite.

WORDS TO KNOW

THE SAME, BUT DIFFERENT

Everyone is familiar with salt. It's white and, of course, it tastes salty. You probably have some in your kitchen. Gold is used in jewelry and is very valuable because of its beautiful color and shine. Although these two minerals are very different in how they look and feel, their atoms are arranged in the same **geometric** pattern—a cube! The difference between gold and salt is that gold is made up of gold atoms and salt is made up of sodium and chlorine atoms. On the flip side, diamonds are the hardest natural substance on Earth, because their atoms are packed closely together. Graphite is gray and smudgy looking—it's what you see as the lead in pencils. You can write with graphite because it is so soft that it rubs off on paper to make a mark. It's hard to imagine two substances more different than diamonds and graphite. But, surprise! Diamonds and graphite are both made of **carbon** atoms. The only difference between diamonds and graphite is the pattern the carbon atoms are arranged in.

element: a pure substance that cannot be broken down into a simpler substance. Everything in the universe is made up of combinations of elements. Oxygen, gold, and carbon are three elements.

oxygen: the most abundant element on the earth, found in air, water, and many rocks.

silicon: an abundant element found in sand, clay, and quartz.

hexagon: a shape with six sides.

WORDS TO KNOW

Different minerals are made of different kinds of atoms. The mineral gold is made of the element gold—only gold atoms. The mineral quartz is made of two elements, a combination of oxygen and silicon atoms. But the kind of atoms that make up a mineral is just part of what makes it unique. Shape is important, too.

If you could see the atoms inside a mineral, you would see the atoms arranged in a pattern—a cube, a hexagon, or another shape. The pattern of atoms is repeated to build a crystal. Sometimes, the pattern repeats only enough to form a very small crystal, but often the pattern repeats enough to form a crystal big enough to see.

HOW DO CRYSTALS GROW?

Minerals, which are almost always made of crystals, grow layer by layer. Crystals form when a liquid cools and the atoms arrange themselves into a solid crystal pattern. Crystals need three things to grow: space, raw materials, and time.

Imagine you are arranging red and blue beads in a simple pattern on a piece of paper. The pattern is red-blue-red-blue. What might limit the amount of the pattern of red and blue beads?

✴ Space. If you fill up the paper, you run out of space. Crystals often grow in cracks, and they can run out of space to grow.

✴ Raw materials. If you run out of blue beads and only have red left, you are missing a raw material and can't continue the pattern. Sometimes, when crystals grow, they run out of a raw material, so that kind of crystal no longer grows—a different one does.

✴ Time. If your mom calls you for dinner, you must stop because you've run out of time. Crystals can run out of time, too. They keep adding layers as long as the liquid is hot enough for the atoms to move around and arrange themselves. But when a substance cools, the atoms can't move around as easily and everything is set in place. Time's up!

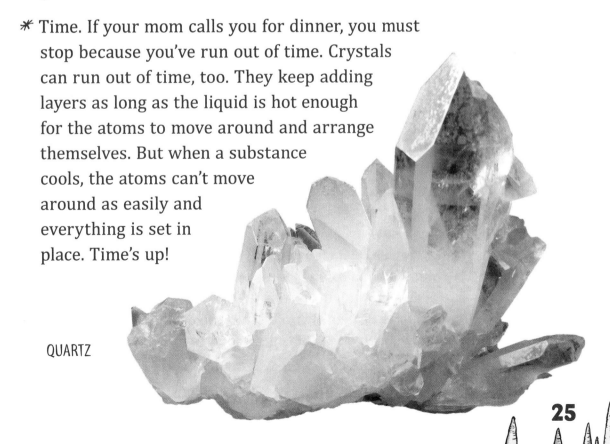

QUARTZ

Check out pictures of minerals and gems at the Smithsonian National Museum of Natural History. What makes them beautiful to us?

🔍 SMITHSONIAN GEM GALLERY

Everyone has habits, and so do minerals. The shape that a mineral's crystals tend to form is called the crystal's habit. Crystals can grow in blocky shapes, as thin, flaky sheets, or as needles. If conditions change, a crystal's habit can change, just like your habits can change. You might brush your teeth every night. But maybe you have a sleepover one night and forget your toothbrush!

Crystals are the same way. Something might change the way the crystal usually grows, so that it forms a different shape. For example, crystals often grow in cracks, where they're closed in on all sides—so their natural shape is distorted.

UNDER PRESSURE!

Pressure is a big deal when you study earth science. What does pressure feel like? If you jump or dive deep into a pool, you can feel the increased pressure of the water on your ears. And the deeper you go, the greater the pressure. If you went 90 miles below the surface of the earth, where diamonds form, you would feel about 50,000 times more pressure. Diamonds can form only under very great pressure, because their atoms are packed so tightly together. How do we find diamonds created so far below the earth's surface? A volcanic eruption often blasts them to the surface.

GEMSTONES

Gemstones are minerals that are especially beautiful, durable, and rare. They often have a bright, vivid color and sparkle. Gemstones are usually cut or polished to show off their beauty.

gemstone: a cut or polished mineral that is beautiful, durable, and rare.

durable: something that lasts for a long time.

rare: something there is not very many or much of.

WORDS ⊕ KNOW

How do you cut a diamond, the hardest substance on Earth? With another diamond, of course! Although diamonds can't be scratched, they do have weak points where they can be cut with special, diamond-coated tools.

DID YOU KNOW?

Ancient Persians thought the earth rested on a huge blue sapphire and the blue sky was its reflection.

A DIAMOND THAT HAS BEEN CUT AND POLISHED

Gems have been used in jewelry for thousands of years. Gemstone jewelry was found in the tomb of Tutankhamun, an Egyptian pharaoh who ruled more than 3,000 years ago!

The next chapter is going to get a little rocky—let's learn about different types of rocks!

?

CONSIDER AND DISCUSS

It's time to consider and discuss: What makes one type of mineral different from another?

PROJECT!

MAKE NEEDLE CRYSTALS

Try growing your own crystals of the mineral epsomite.

SUPPLIES

* 1 cup Epsom salts
* black construction paper
* magnifying glass
* scissors
* pie pan or cookie sheet with edges
* large measuring cup
* 1 cup hot tap water
* food coloring (optional)
* science journal

1 Place a few Epsom salt grains on the black paper and look at them closely with the magnifying glass. What shape are the grains?

2 Cut the paper into whatever shape you like, such as a snowflake or heart. Place the paper into the pie pan or cookie sheet. Make sure the paper fits completely within it.

3 Slowly add the Epsom salts into the hot water, stirring constantly. Keep stirring until all of the Epsom salts are dissolved if possible. Add food coloring if you like.

4 Pour the solution over the paper. Place the pan in a warm place such as a sunny window. Or, with an adult's help, place it in a 200-degree-Fahrenheit oven (93 degrees Celsius) for 15 minutes or so—but watch to make sure the solution doesn't dry out too much.

5 After crystals start to grow, examine them. What kind of habit do your crystals have? Cubic? Spiky? Where do you think the crystals came from? Draw what you see in your science journal.

THINK ABOUT IT: What could you do to stop crystals from growing? What do crystals need to grow? How is the growth of a crystal different from a plant growing?

MAKE A CRYSTAL GEODE

Geodes are hollow rocks that contain crystals inside. Try making your own geodes!

1 Gently crack the eggs in half. Pull apart the two sides of the eggshell and dispose of the inside. Gently wash the inside of the eggshell and let dry. Wash your hands thoroughly to remove any raw egg.

2 When the eggshells are dry, use the Q-tip to spread a thin layer of glue on the inside of the eggshells. Sprinkle alum powder onto the glue until the glue is covered in powder. Let dry overnight.

3 Pour about one cup hot tap water into a cup. Add a spoonful of alum and stir to dissolve. Keep adding alum a spoonful at a time until it stops dissolving; it should hold several tablespoons. Add a few drops of food coloring.

4 Place an eggshell half into the solution so that the eggshell is submerged and the opening is facing up. Repeat with more eggshells and solution if desired.

5 Set in a place it won't be disturbed and cover with a cloth. Leave it overnight or longer. Remove the eggshell and let dry.

SUPPLIES

* eggs
* glue
* brush or Q-tip
* hot water
* cup
* alum powder (found in the grocery store with spices)
* food coloring

TAKE IT FURTHER! Try this again, but put the cup into the refrigerator to let the crystals form. How does it change the crystals that grow? Does this tell you anything about what kind of environment is best for very large crystals to grow?

PROJECT!

SALT CRYSTAL MODEL

SUPPLIES

* toothpicks
* red and green gumdrops
* grains of salt
* magnifying glass

The salt that you put on your food comes from a mineral in the earth. Like all minerals, its atoms are arranged in a pattern. Create a simple model of a salt crystal.

1 Make a square of four gumdrops, with each gumdrop connected by a toothpick to a different color gumdrop. The gumdrops represent the atoms and the toothpicks represent the bonds between them. The red gumdrops represent sodium atoms and the green gumdrops are chlorine atoms.

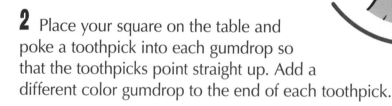

CAN YOU HELP ME DIG UP THIS BIG CRYSTAL?

Of quartz!

2 Place your square on the table and poke a toothpick into each gumdrop so that the toothpicks point straight up. Add a different color gumdrop to the end of each toothpick.

3 Connect the upper layer of gumdrops with toothpicks to make a box with gumdrops in the corners. Each gumdrop should be connected to three gumdrops of the opposite color.

4 Expand your model by adding more toothpicks on one side of the square and then attaching gumdrops of the opposite color. Draw a picture of your model in your science journal.

··· DID YOU KNOW? ···

More than 3,000 different minerals exist on Earth, but only about 100 are commonly found.

STRUVITE CRYSTALS UNDER A MICROSCOPE
CREDIT: SUSANA SECRETARIAT (CC BY 2.0)

5 Sprinkle a few grains of salt on a dark piece of paper and look at them closely with a magnifying glass. Is the shape of the salt crystals like the shape of your salt model? Why do you think they're similar?

THINK ABOUT IT: To show how many atoms are in one grain of salt, it would take 100 quintillion more squares than in your model. One grain of salt has more atoms than there are people on Earth, stars in our galaxy, or grains of sand on a beach!

GROW SOME ROCK CANDY

In this activity you will see how sugar crystals grow.

> **Caution:** Have an adult do steps 3–5.
> Sugar syrup is extremely hot.

1 Place a few sugar crystals onto black paper and look at the grains closely, using a magnifying glass if you have one. What shape are the grains? Make a drawing in your science journal.

2 Tie one end of the string to the button and wrap the other end around the pencil. Put the pencil over the opening of the jar so that the string hangs down into the jar. Adjust the length of the string so that the button is just above the bottom of the jar.

3 Pour about 1 cup of water into the saucepan and add the sugar. Have an adult heat the sugar water until it boils, stirring just until the sugar dissolves.

4 Without stirring, cook the sugar syrup over medium heat for 3 minutes. Remove the saucepan from the heat and let cool for 2 minutes. Carefully pour the syrup into the jar to just below the brim. If extra sugar is on the bottom of the saucepan, do not pour it into the jar.

SUPPLIES

* ✳ 2 cups sugar
* ✳ black paper
* ✳ magnifying glass (optional)
* ✳ cotton string
* ✳ button
* ✳ pencil
* ✳ tall jar
* ✳ water
* ✳ saucepan
* ✳ food coloring (optional)

DID YOU KNOW?

The Hope Diamond is perhaps the most famous diamond in the world. It was found in India and is now on display at the Smithsonian Museum in Washington, DC. In fact, if you visit the Smithsonian, you can walk right up and look at it (it's behind protective glass, of course)! The Hope Diamond is unusual because it is blue, which is a rare color for a diamond. It has belonged to King Louis XIV of France and King George IV of England and has mysteriously vanished and been found again more than once!

5 Using a potholder, move the jar to a warm place where you can easily see it but it won't be disturbed.

6 Be patient! Watch the crystal grow each day, but don't touch the jar. In your science journal, record how big the crystal is each day. If no crystal forms, or if the whole glass of syrup turns into a solid lump, you may have stirred it while it was boiling. Try again!

THINK ABOUT IT: What shape are the crystals? Do they look like the sugar crystals you observed at the beginning? How are they alike? How are they different? How does the size of the crystals change each day? Why do you think the size changes?

CHAPTER 3

IGNEOUS ROCKS

What happens when you heat chocolate? It melts, of course. When you cool the chocolate, it becomes solid again. The same thing happens with rocks, except that rocks need much more heat to melt—about four times more heat than you need to bake cookies.

Where does it get that hot? Remember the layers of the earth we discussed in Chapter 1? If you could tunnel toward the center of the earth, it would get hotter and hotter. About 25 miles beneath the surface, it's hot enough to melt rocks. Magma is the molten rock beneath the surface of the earth.

? INVESTIGATE!

How do igneous rocks form?

When magma forms, it slowly bubbles up to the earth's surface. The closer it gets to the surface, the cooler the magma becomes, and eventually becomes solid. Rocks that form from cooling magma are called igneous rocks.

There are two types of igneous rocks. Let's explore them.

INTRUSIVE ROCKS

When magma cools and hardens before it reaches the surface of the earth, it forms intrusive igneous rocks. Magma can form deep underground in huge blobs many miles across. As these blobs rise and cool, they form large areas of rock.

MOUNT RUSHMORE IS CARVED OUT OF INTRUSIVE IGNEOUS ROCK!

ROCKS AND MINERALS!

Igneous rock is very hard. As softer rock above and around it wears away, the igneous rock is left standing at the surface. Long mountain chains are often intrusive igneous rocks formed from huge blobs of magma.

EXTRUSIVE ROCKS

Magma that rises all the way to the surface of the earth is called lava. Lava erupts from volcanoes and cools to form extrusive igneous rocks.

CRATER LAKE VOLCANO IN OREGON IS EXTRUSIVE IGNEOUS ROCK

SNOW IN JULY

In 1815, the Tambora volcano in Indonesia had the most powerful eruption in recorded history. Thousands of people died. The volcano released so much ash and gas that it blocked some sunlight and caused the entire earth to become cooler. The next year was called "the year without a summer," because it snowed year-round in Europe and North America. Imagine snow in July!

In most volcanoes, such as the ones active in Hawaii, the lava is runny and slowly bubbles out. These volcanoes are dangerous, but not as dangerous as explosive volcanoes, such as Mount St. Helens in Washington state. Those really blow their tops!

When explosive volcanoes erupt, a high-speed and very dangerous mass of lava, hot ash, pieces of rock, and gas can travel downhill up to 150 miles per hour. That's a lot faster than cars travel on the highway!

Why are some volcanoes runny and some explosive? Runny volcanoes have thin lava similar to salad dressing. Gases can escape easily before the lava reaches the surface. Runny volcanoes are usually located where tectonic plates are pulling apart. Many of them are under the oceans.

CAREER CONNECTION: VOLCANOLOGISTS

Volcanologists are scientists who study volcanoes. They want to understand how volcanoes work. They also want to be able to predict what volcanoes will do, so they can warn people living near volcanoes before eruptions. Their dangerous job includes taking samples of volcanic gases and lava. When working around volcanoes, volcanologists protect themselves by wearing suits made from a special fabric that reflects heat and doesn't catch fire—lava can be as hot as 1,800 degrees Fahrenheit (982 degrees Celsius). They also wear helmets and hoods with special glasses to protect their eyes from the super-bright lava and wear breathing masks because of harmful gases.

Explosive volcanoes have thick and pasty lava similar to toothpaste. Gases build up until they explode when the lava reaches the surface. Explosive volcanoes are usually located around the edges of tectonic plates where one plate is pushing under another. The rock that cools after an explosive volcano is extrusive igneous rock.

BIG GRAINS, LITTLE GRAINS, NO GRAINS

When magma cools, the atoms arrange themselves into patterns that form crystals.

You can see footage of a volcanic eruption in this video. Do you think this produced intrusive or extrusive rock? Or both?

🔍 NYT VOLCANO HAWAII

Magma can take thousands, even millions, of years to cool and form intrusive rocks. Because of this, the atoms have lots of time to arrange themselves into layers that form large crystals. Rocks with large crystals that you can see with your eyes are called coarse-grained.

When magma cools quickly, as it does when a volcano erupts and releases lava, the atoms have little time to arrange themselves. The crystals that form are too small to see without a microscope. Rocks such as these take only weeks or days to form and are called fine-grained.

Sometimes, the lava cools so fast that it can't form crystals at all. When this happens, the magma produces volcanic glass.

Here are some common igneous rocks.

DID YOU KNOW?

Some islands, such as those that make up the state of Hawaii and the country of Iceland, are made up entirely of volcanic rocks.

* **Granite** is an intrusive rock, so it is coarse-grained. Many buildings, kitchen countertops, and statues are made of granite. It is white, gray, or pale pink in color. Granite is made of quartz, feldspar, and mica. It can look sparkly in the sunlight because tiny bits of mica reflect light.

✳ **Basalt** is an extrusive rock, so it is very fine-grained. Basalt is dark brownish-gray and is made of feldspar, pyroxene, and a small amount of quartz. These dense minerals make basalt heavy and give it its dark color. Basalt forms when magma rises to the surface and erupts as lava from volcanoes. You can often see little holes where gas was trapped. When basalt lava cools, it shrinks and cracks. Sometimes, the cracks are very regular and can result in columns with six sides.

DID YOU KNOW?

Basalt covers more of the earth's surface than any other rock because it forms almost all the oceanic crust. If you dug under the thin layer of **sediment** at the bottom of the oceans, you'd find basalt.

BASALT COLUMNS MAKE UP GIANT'S CAUSEWAY IN NORTHERN IRELAND.

INSTANT ISLAND

On November 14, 1963, fishermen in the Atlantic Ocean south of Iceland noticed smoke rising from the water. By the next morning, a land mass later named Surtsey Island had appeared! After four days, it was 197 feet high. Where did it come from? Surtsey Island formed when plates in the earth's crust pulled apart and magma from deep within the earth bubbled up. This is how the country of Iceland formed!

* **Obsidian** has sharp edges and a surface that looks like glass—because it is glass! But you can't see through obsidian because it contains chemicals that give it a dark color. Ancient people used obsidian to make weapons. Even now, people use obsidian to make scalpel blades for surgery because it has very thin, sharp edges.

* **Pumice** is another kind of glassy rock. It's usually white, with lots of holes. When magma rises fast, it can be a frothy mixture of gases and liquid rock. Pumice comes from this frothy mixture, with the gas bubbles causing the holes. Pumice is used in construction materials.

WHAT DID THE MAMA VOLCANO SAY TO THE PAPA VOLCANO WHEN HE GAVE HER FLOWERS?

HOW LAVA-LY!

Igneous rocks aren't the only rocks on the planet! In the next chapter, we'll meet a different type of rock.

? CONSIDER AND DISCUSS

It's time to consider and discuss:
How do igneous rocks form?

MAKE BASALT COLUMNS

Scientists use cornstarch and water to study how basalt cools and forms columns. You can, too!

1 Mix equal parts of cornstarch and water in the pie dish until it is about half full. Stir well.

2 Set the pie dish under a bright light for one week or until it is completely dry. The light should be several inches above the dish. You could also use a sunny windowsill. What do you see? Keep it under the light until you see much finer cracks at the top. The longer it dries, the better.

3 Hold up the pie dish and look at the bottom. Do you see any shapes? Carefully pry up pieces of cornstarch and see if it formed columns. How are they shaped? If you don't see columns, let the cornstarch dry out more.

4 In your science journal, draw a picture of the columns looking from the side. Then, draw a **cross section**. A cross section is a view that cuts across something. If you hold the pie dish above your head, you have a cross section view. How are your cornstarch columns like basalt columns?

THINK ABOUT IT: Most liquids—except water—shrink when they cool and become solid. Lava does, too. Do you think that has anything to do with the columns in basalt and your cornstarch? Have you ever seen mud when it dries? Does it have cracks?

WORDS TO KNOW

cross section: a surface or shape that is exposed by making a straight cut through something.

PROJECT!

LAVA GAS!

Lava has gas trapped in it. How does it compare to the gas in soda that some people drink?

1 Open one can of soda and take a few sips.

2 Pour some of the soda into a glass and let it sit for a few hours. Taste the soda. Is the fizz different? Why do you think it tastes less fizzy?

···· DID YOU KNOW? ·······

In May 2018, on the island of Hawaii, the Kīlauea volcano erupted with 1 billion cubic yards of lava—enough to fill at least 320,000 Olympic-size swimming pools! The lava destroyed 716 houses, covered 30 miles of roads, and created 875 acres of new land by lava flowing into the ocean.

3 Go outside, shake the second can of soda, point it away from you, and open it. What happens?

THINK ABOUT IT: Soda has dissolved gas in it, just like lava. When the gas has lots of time to escape from the lava as it rises to the surface, it's "flat" like the soda you let sit out—it loses its fizz. If plenty of gas is trapped in the lava and doesn't have much time to escape, it's like the soda that you've shaken. When the pressure is finally released, look out!

MAKE PUMICE COOKIES

Have you ever eaten a rock? These cookies aren't exactly rocks, but they look like the volcanic rock called pumice. Make these cookies on a cool, dry day. In hot, humid weather, they won't dry properly.

CAUTION: Have an adult help with the oven and knife.

1 Preheat the oven to 250 degrees Fahrenheit (121 degrees Celsius) and put the oven rack in the center position. Line a cookie sheet with wax paper.

2 Hold an egg lightly with one hand, and with the other hand, crack the eggshell firmly with the butter knife.

3 Pull the eggshell apart without letting the yolk fall into the bowl. Pour the yolk back and forth between the eggshell halves, letting the egg white fall into the bowl. Keep the yolk in the shell and be careful that it doesn't break. When all the white is in the bowl, put the yolk into the other bowl to use for another cooking project. Pour the white from the small bowl into the large bowl, so that if you break a yolk on the next egg, you won't ruin the whole batch. Repeat this process for the rest of the eggs.

4 Add the cream of tartar or vinegar to the egg whites in the large bowl. Beat the mixture with an electric mixer on high until the egg whites get foamy and form soft peaks that gently flop over when you remove the beaters.

SUPPLIES

* cookie sheet
* wax paper
* 6 eggs at room temperature
* butter knife
* two small bowls
* large metal or glass bowl
* ¼ teaspoon cream of tartar or white vinegar
* electric mixer
* ½ cup sugar
* ¼ teaspoon vanilla (optional)

5 Gradually add the sugar and vanilla and keep beating just until the whites are shiny, smooth, and stand up in peaks about 2 inches high. This is meringue!

6 Drop big blobs of the meringue onto the wax paper on the cookie sheet and bake for 1 hour 30 minutes. The meringue should look dry, stiff, and very light brown. Turn off the oven and let the meringue cookies cool completely in the oven before you take them out. Cool for at least 1 hour.

7 Clean up carefully! Don't lick the bowl because raw eggs can make you sick. For the same reason, use paper towels to wipe up any spilled raw egg, then throw the paper in the trash.

8 Once the cookies are cool, break one in half and look at the broken edge. What do you see? Is your "pumice" lighter than other cookies the same size? Why do you think that is?

THINK ABOUT IT: Why do you think pumice is the only rock that can float on water?

PROJECT!

MAKE YOUR OWN FOAMY VOLCANO

Remember, models are one way scientists make observations. Make your own volcano and see what it does!

1 Set the bottle on the tray. Without blocking the opening of the bottle, shape the Play-Doh or crumpled aluminum foil around the bottle into a cone. If you want, place pebbles around the base of the cone, and add twigs, flowers, or pine cones to the Play-Doh or aluminum to create trees, flowers, and boulders.

2 Use the funnel to fill the bottle about ⅔ full of warm water. Add several drops of red food coloring and two drops of yellow food coloring, or any other color you'd like. Add 3 tablespoons of baking soda and a squirt of dish soap.

3 Use the funnel to quickly pour in vinegar to just below the rim. Remove the funnel and watch your volcano erupt!

THINK ABOUT IT: The vinegar and baking soda have a chemical reaction that produces gas. The gas builds up and bubbles out of the volcano. Although real volcanoes don't have vinegar or baking soda, they have other chemicals that react and produce gas that builds up.

PROJECT!

MODEL MAGMA PLUMES

What makes plumes of magma rise? Try this experiment to find out.

SUPPLIES

* ✳ 1 cup tap water
* ✳ clear glass or plastic jar
* ✳ ½ cup cooking oil
* ✳ food coloring (optional)
* ✳ salt in a shaker

1 Pour the water into the jar until it is a little more than half full.

2 Pour the oil into the jar and let the water and oil separate and settle. Add food coloring if you want.

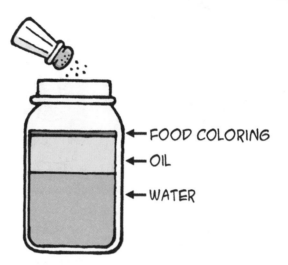

← FOOD COLORING

← OIL

← WATER

3 Shake the salt onto the oil for several seconds or until some of the oil begins to sink. When the oil begins to rise again, shake salt onto it again. Keep going as long as you like! What do you notice happening? Record your observations in your science journal.

THINK ABOUT IT: Oil is less dense than water, so it floats. But salt is denser than either oil or water, so it sinks. And when you shake it onto the oil, at first it carries the oil with it. But soon, the salt dissolves in the water. Without the salt to weigh it down, the oil rises again—until you shake more salt on it! But what about magma plumes? A hot material is less dense than the same material that is colder. Plumes of magma rise because they are hotter than the surrounding rock.

CHAPTER 4

SEDIMENTARY ROCKS

Everyone loves the beach! The crashing waves and the miles of sand make for great fun. Sand is also central to the second major rock type—sedimentary rock. This rock comes from sediment, or tiny particles that are pressed tightly together.

Standing on a sandy beach, you're looking at the ingredients for future sedimentary rocks. To understand how most sedimentary rocks form, you must understand how erosion got the sand to the beach in the first place.

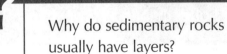

? INVESTIGATE!

Why do sedimentary rocks usually have layers?

sedimentary rock:
rock formed from
sediment, the remains of
plants or animals, or the
evaporation of seawater.

WORDS ⏍ KNOW

EROSION

Imagine that you're a huge boulder high on a mountain. For the first few thousand years or so, you think nothing can change you. But slowly, rain, wind, and ice break you down.

One winter, you crack a little bit in a few places. Water drips into these cracks and freezes, and the cracks get bigger. Maybe wind knocks a rock against you, breaking off a piece. Before you know it—after many more thousands of years—you're just a pile of smaller rocks tumbling down the mountainside.

During a rainstorm, you're swept into a stream. Here, water breaks you down into even smaller rocks and smooths your sharp edges. Eventually, the small pieces of rock become sediment, such as pebbles or sand. You might settle at the bottom of a river, be carried out to the ocean, or be blown by the wind.

One thing is certain— you've been eroded! You have separated from the boulder you started as, and have traveled far and wide, getting smaller and smaller.

EROSION CAUSED THIS UNUSUAL ROCK FORMATION.

clastic sedimentary rock: rock that forms from rock fragments, or clasts, pressed together.

clast: a rock fragment such as a pebble, sand, or clay.

deposit: to place.

WORDS ᴛᴏ KNOW

CLASTIC SEDIMENTARY ROCKS

The most common sedimentary rocks on Earth are clastic sedimentary rocks. These are formed when sediments—also called clasts—are pressed together into rock.

How does this happen? Wind or water deposits sediment in layers. As the layers are buried farther and farther below the surface, they heat up. Often, water containing minerals soaks into the layers. When the sediment becomes hotter, the water dries, and the minerals left behind "glue" the sediment together. Then, pressure from above changes soft sediment— such as beach sand—into hard rocks. This process takes millions of years.

THIS SANDSTONE CLIFF IS MADE OF CLASTIC SEDIMENTARY ROCK.

ORGANIC SEDIMENTARY ROCKS

Organic sedimentary rocks are formed from the remains of plants and animals. For example, limestone is a pale tan or gray organic sedimentary rock made mostly of the mineral calcite.

Calcite is organic. It comes from the shells of sea creatures. These animals absorb mineral particles from the water around them to form their shells. After the animals die, their shells fall to the ocean floor, where they are eventually pressed together into limestone.

LIMESTONE CLIFFS ON THE ISLAND OF CORSICA

Coal is a black or dark brown rock. We use coal to generate electricity. Like limestone, coal is formed from the remains of living things.

More than 300 million years ago—even before the dinosaurs lived—plant-filled swamps covered the earth. When the plants died, they sank into the swamps and were covered with sand and mud. As time passed, more and more sediment buried the plant remains. Eventually, this turned into coal.

CLIMATE CHANGE

Have you heard **climate change** mentioned in the news recently? **Climate** change refers to the way the earth is heating up. The temperature is rising because there are a lot of **greenhouse gases** in the **atmosphere**. These gases act as an invisible blanket that traps heat close to the planet's surface. One of these gases, carbon dioxide, seeps into the atmosphere when coal is burned to make power. That's why many power plants are switching to natural gas instead of coal—natural gas releases less carbon dioxide. People are also exploring other ways of making electricity, such as using the wind and the sun. Right now, the earth is warming faster than ever before in history! That means a lot of things will change. Many **organisms** might not be able to **adapt** fast enough to the changing climate.

CHEMICAL SEDIMENTARY ROCKS

Chemical sedimentary rocks are formed from solutions. A solution is a liquid with a mineral dissolved in it, such as salt water. When the liquid evaporates, the minerals are left behind. Chemical sedimentary rocks usually form when shallow inland seas slowly dry up, leaving minerals behind.

chemical sedimentary rock: sedimentary rock that forms when water that contains dissolved minerals evaporates and leaves behind the mineral deposits.

solution: one substance dissolved into another.

evaporate: to convert from liquid to gas.

WORDS ⊚ KNOW

While limestone is often an organic sedimentary rock, it can also be a chemical sedimentary rock. Seawater contains dissolved calcite, so limestone can form when seawater evaporates.

The clear or white mineral called halite—also known as rock salt— forms when seawater evaporates. Seawater contains a lot of salt— that's why you can't drink it!

··· DID YOU KNOW? ···

The Dead Sea is so salty that it leaves deposits of salt on its shores and bottom.

SALTY HOTEL

The Salt Palace and Spa is in the Uyuni Salt Flats in Bolivia. The entire hotel, including the furniture, is made of salt! Long ago, the Uyuni Salt Flats were salt water lakes. As time passed, the lakes evaporated and the salt was left behind.

Check out this National Geographic video to see the Uyuni Salt Flats and hotel.

🔎 NAT GEO SALT HOTEL

ROCKS AND MINERALS!

Gypsum is another mineral found in seawater. When seawater evaporates from shallow inland seas, it leaves behind this soft, white or transparent mineral. People have mined gypsum since ancient times. Today, gypsum is used to build walls inside houses.

FOSSILS

How do we know about creatures that lived on Earth before any humans? Fossils! Fossils are the remains of ancient plants and animals preserved in sedimentary rock.

Fossils include shells, bones, imprints, tracks, and, occasionally, an entire organism. Fossils don't form every time an organism dies. First, sediment must bury the remains of an organism. Then, water with minerals dissolved in it must seep into tiny pores—such as those found in bones—in the organism.

SALLY SELLS SEASHELLS

The famous tongue twister is based on Mary Anning, an early British fossil collector. Born in 1799 in Lyme Regis, England, Mary hunted for fossils and sold them to keep the family from going broke after her father died. When she was only 12, Mary discovered the first Ichthyosaurus, a massive, fish-like reptile that weighed up to 1 ton! Later, she found a fossil of a plesiosaur, another enormous marine reptile. Her work was so important to paleontology that she was made an honorary member of the Geological Society of London, which did not admit women as members until almost 60 years later.

A FOSSILIZED FISH
CREDIT: JAMES ST. JOHN (CC BY 2.0)

With heat and pressure, the minerals and sediments turn into rock. A fossil is made!

Most fossils come from ocean creatures, especially shellfish, and are almost always found in sedimentary rocks. That's because in the ocean, sediment quickly covers shells and bones. On land, the remains of animals usually rot away before they can be preserved.

WATSON: HOLMES! WHAT KIND OF ROCK IS THIS?

SHERLOCK HOLMES: SEDIMENTARY, MY DEAR WATSON.

Rocks can tell you a lot about the place they were found. In the next chapter, we'll learn about the third kind of rock!

?

CONSIDER AND DISCUSS

It's time to consider and discuss: Why do sedimentary rocks usually have layers?

PROJECT!

MAKE A MINI-CANYON

SUPPLIES

* 5 colors of play clay
* rolling pin
* cardboard about 12 inches square
* thin wire

Rivers sometimes cut through many layers of rock. Try this activity to see how a canyon might form.

1 Roll out each color of clay about a quarter-inch thick. Stack the layers of clay onto the cardboard. These are like the layers of rock.

2 Imagine a "river" runs through the clay, parallel to one side of the cardboard. Run your fingernail lightly across the top of the clay to show the direction of the river.

3 Holding the wire taut and parallel to the table and to the river, make two vertical cuts through the top layer of clay. Peel away the slab of the top layer of clay to reveal the layer of clay underneath.

4 On the next layer of clay, make two cuts at an angle. Place the wire at the bottom of the top layer of clay and pull it down and toward the river until you reach the next layer. Repeat on the other side of the river, then peel away this layer.

5 Continue cutting away layers until you reach the cardboard.

THINK ABOUT IT: The layers of clay where you cut straight down are called cliff-forming rocks. The layers where you cut at an angle are called slope-forming rocks. Do you think the cliff-forming rocks are harder or softer than the slope-forming rocks? Why do you think you made the cuts parallel to the direction of the river?

PROJECT!

MAKE A SEDIMENTARY ROCK

While sedimentary rock takes millions of years to form, you can make your own in much less time!

1 With an adult's help, cut off the top of the soda bottle using the scissors.

2 Mix about ½ cup sand with ½ cup plaster of Paris in the bowl. Put the mixture into the empty bottle.

3 Repeat step 2 with other sediment, such as gravel and pebbles. Mix the same amount of plaster of Paris and sediment together before putting it into the bottle. You can also add a layer of just plaster of Paris. If you like, push seashells into a layer.

4 Slowly pour water into the soda bottle until it just covers the top layer. Wait one or more days until everything is dry. Cut away the soda bottle. You now have sedimentary rock!

PLASTER OF PARIS

SUPPLIES

* scissors
* empty 2-liter soda bottle, label removed
* large bowl and spoon
* measuring cup
* sand
* plaster of Paris, from a hardware or craft store
* pieces of gravel, smaller than a penny
* pebbles of various sizes
* one or more seashells (optional)
* water

THINK ABOUT IT: Which kind of sedimentary rock do you think the layer with sand represents? What about gravel or pebbles? What about the layer with seashells? Read the descriptions of rock types for clues. Which of your rock layers is the oldest layer?

57

PROJECT!

MAKE STALACTITES AND STALAGMITES

SUPPLIES

* 2 cups hot tap water
* Epsom salts
* cotton or wool string
* 4 paper clips
* dish

Rainwater sometimes contains dissolved gases that make it acidic. When acidic rainwater trickles down to limestone beneath the surface of the earth, it dissolves the limestone, eventually creating caves. Sometimes, these caves contain stalactites and stalagmites. When rainwater seeps through limestone, the minerals forming the limestone dissolve in the water. As the water drips down, it leaves behind traces of limestone. Drop by drop, huge stalactites and stalagmites form. Stalactites are formations that hang down from the ceilings of caves (the word stalactite has a "c" for ceiling) and stalagmites rise from the ground (think "g" for ground). Try forming your own stalactites and stalagmites.

1 Fill the cups about half full of hot water. Stir in Epsom salts until no more will dissolve.

2 Cut about 18 inches of string. Tie two paper clips to each end and place the entire string in one cup.

3 Place the cups about 1 foot apart with the dish in between, somewhere they won't be disturbed.

WORDS ⦿ KNOW

acidic: from acids, which are chemical compounds that taste sour, bitter, or tart. Examples are vinegar and lemon juice. Water also contains some acid.

stalactite: a cave formation that looks like an icicle hanging from the ceiling.

stalagmite: a cave formation projecting up from the floor, often underneath a stalactite.

WHICH FORMATIONS ARE STALACTITES AND WHICH ARE STALAGMITES?

4 Pull the string out and drape it between the cups. The paper clips should rest in the bottom of each cup. The string should droop slightly but shouldn't touch the dish.

5 Check the project each day. Have any stalactites or stalagmites formed? Draw a picture in your science journal.

THINK ABOUT IT: What happened to the Epsom salts when you put them in hot water? How did your stalactites or stalagmites form? What do you think they're made of?

PROJECT!

WHERE'S THE WATER?

SUPPLIES

* ✴ small mixing bowl
* ✴ hot tap water
* ✴ table salt
* ✴ small and large spoon
* ✴ shallow baking pan

Chemical sedimentary rocks form through evaporation. See for yourself!

1 Fill the bowl about two-thirds full of hot tap water. Scoop small spoonfuls of salt into the water. Stir the mixture with the large spoon after you add each spoonful. Keep adding salt until it doesn't dissolve anymore.

2 Pour the mixture into the baking pan. Set the pan in a place where it won't be disturbed, ideally on a warm windowsill. In your science journal, predict what you think will happen.

3 Check the pan after a day. Is there still water? Do you see any crystals forming? Keep checking until all the water has evaporated.

····· DID YOU KNOW? ·····

White Sands National Monument in New Mexico has the largest gypsum sand dunes in the world. It formed long ago when there was a huge shallow sea within North America, which then evaporated, leaving behind the gypsum. Now, it's a desert!

SAND DUNES MADE OF GYPSUM

THINK ABOUT IT: Where did the salt go when you mixed it with the water? Where did the water go after a few days? What do you think would happen if you added hot water to your salt crystals again? Try it and see if you're right.

PROJECT!

EROSION

Wind, water, and ice can erode rocks. Try this activity to get an idea of two ways a rock can erode.

SUPPLIES

* bar of soap
* sponge
* sugar cubes
* handful of gravel
* coffee can with lid
* paper
* handful of gravel
* several sugar cubes

1 Place the bar of soap on the sponge. Set the sponge under the faucet of the kitchen or bathroom sink. Let your family know what you're doing!

2 Turn the faucet on so that it slowly drips water onto the soap.

3 Add the sugar cubes and gravel to the coffee can and shake it vigorously for about 5 minutes. What do you think will happen to the gravel and sugar? Open the can and pour the contents onto paper. Do the sugar cubes and gravel look different? Which changed more, the sugar cubes or the gravel? Why?

4 After about an hour, check back on your soap. Does it look different? If not, keep the soap under the dripping faucet longer. What happens to it? How is this similar to erosion?

THINK ABOUT IT: How did the dripping water change the appearance of the soap? Would it take water less or more time to erode rock compared with soap? Why? What would happen if you increased or decreased how fast the water drips? Try it and see if your predictions are correct.

WALK THROUGH TIME

The earth formed a very long time ago. It's really hard to imagine! Compared to when life first appeared, humans have been around for only a very, very short period. Try this activity to get some idea of how long the earth and its creatures have been here.

Grab a friend or adult who's good at counting. Pick a place where you can walk for 10 minutes or so without stopping, such as a walking path or your school playground. Start walking and count out loud together for every step you take. When you complete the steps listed below, name the step and say what happened at that time. Then, keep walking and counting. Each step you take represents 10 million years!

Step 1	Earth formed	4,600 million years ago
Step 40	Oldest mineral	a zircon found in Australia is 4,400 million years old
Step 60	Oldest rock	a rock found in Canada is 4,000 million years old
Step 95	Oldest fossils	blue-green **algae** fossils probably appeared about 3,650 million years ago in Greenland
Step 250	First cells with **nucleus**	about 2,100 million years ago, possibly earlier

WORDS ⦿ KNOW

algae: a simple organism found in water that is like a plant but without roots, stems, or leaves.

nucleus: the central part of the cell that controls how it functions.

PROJECT!

Step 390	First sponges	about 700 million years ago
Step 405	First abundant life	Earth teemed with life starting about 542 million years ago
Step 435	"The Great Dying"	major **extinction** killing up to 96 percent of life about 250 million years ago
Step 436	First dinosaurs	almost 230 million years ago
Step 438	First **mammals**	about 225 million years ago
Step 453	Dinosaurs extinct	65 million years ago
Step 455	First dogs	about 54 million years ago
Step 459 ½	First human ancestors	about 5.5 million years ago
Step 459 ¾	First humans	almost 3 million years ago

THINK ABOUT IT: Whew! That was a lot of step counting, and humans came into the picture only at the very, very end of your walk.

WORDS TO KNOW

extinction: the death of an entire species so that it no longer exists.

mammal: a type of animal, such as a human, dog, or cat. Mammals are born live, feed milk to their young, and usually have hair or fur covering most of their skin.

DID YOU KNOW?

Even poop can be a fossil! Fossilized poop is called coprolite. It can help scientists learn about an ancient animal's diet.

PROJECT!

ICE WEATHERING

Ice is a pretty powerful force—so powerful it can break rock! See for yourself in this project.

1 Fill the plastic cup about half full of water and mark the water level on the cup. Place the cup upright in the freezer for two days, keeping the water level.

2 Pull out the cup, which should now be solid ice. What level is the ice compared with the water level? Why?

3 Fill the glass jar with water to the very top—make sure there is no air. Screw the lid on tightly. Place the jar into the plastic bag and seal it. Place the bag in the freezer for at least two days. What do you think will happen? Record your prediction in your science journal.

4 Carefully pull out the plastic bag. What happened to the jar? Did the jar break? Why or why not? If the glass didn't break, you may not have filled the jar full enough. Try adding more water up to the very top and place in the freezer for one more day. Be careful when handling the bag with the broken glass!

THINK ABOUT IT: Most liquids decrease in volume when they become solids. Water is unusual. When it freezes and becomes a solid, the volume increases. What do you think happens when water seeps into cracks in rocks and then later freezes as temperatures drop?

WORDS TO KNOW

volume: the amount of space occupied by something.

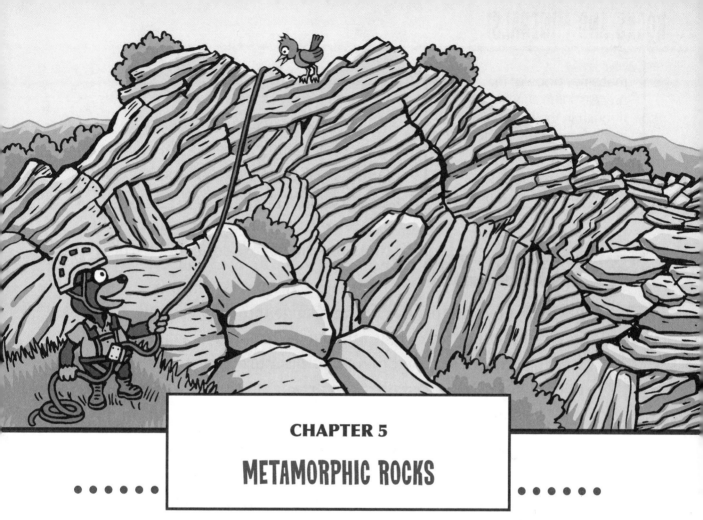

CHAPTER 5

METAMORPHIC ROCKS

Have you ever seen a caterpillar change into a butterfly? It's an amazing change—if you didn't see it, you might not believe that such a delicate creature could come from a fat caterpillar. The caterpillar went through metamorphosis, **or completely changed its nature and appearance.**

That's what the third kind of rocks, metamorphic rocks, are all about—change. Metamorphic rocks form when heat or pressure changes existing rocks into new rocks. Metamorphic rocks are often very hard and dense rocks. The pressure that creates them packs their atoms closely together.

? INVESTIGATE!

Why don't we notice when rocks break down and form new rocks?

When heat or pressure is applied to rocks, they change. Deep in the earth's mantle, a lot of heat and pressure melts rock into magma. Close to the earth's surface, a little heat and pressure glues grains together into sedimentary rock.

But there's an in-between way of changing rock, too. Rocks can change into a completely different kind of rock while staying solid as they change. When rocks are exposed to heat or pressure, the atoms in the minerals slowly recrystallize—rearranging themselves into new crystals.

The crystals may get larger or smaller. Sometimes, completely new minerals form. The kind of rock that forms depends on the amount of heat or pressure and on the minerals that were in the original rocks.

CLAY

-SQUISH-

CLAY STAYS SQUISHED (LIKE META-MORPHIC ROCK)

What happens if you squish down clay, then take your hand off? It doesn't spring back up—it stays squished. Metamorphic rocks are the same way. The new minerals and the new crystal structures "lock in" at the higher temperatures and pressures and usually stay that way, even as the rocks cool. Let's take a look at the different kinds of metamorphic rock.

TIME TO METAMORPHOSE

Sometimes, blobs of super-hot lava rise through the earth's crust and "cook" the surrounding rock. This is called contact metamorphism. The igneous rocks that form from the cool magma have a ring of metamorphic rocks around them. The ring can be just an inch or two wide or miles across.

Regional metamorphism happens when plates crash into each other and form long mountain chains at the boundaries. There's lots of heat and pressure at these sites—perfect for making metamorphic rocks! The rocks that form in this way happen across large areas. They are soft and often fold as they get pushed and shoved by other rocks around them.

contact metamorphism: metamorphism that happens when rocks encounter hot magma.

regional metamorphism: metamorphism that happens at convergent tectonic plate boundaries.

WORDS ⊚ KNOW

THIS CLIFFSIDE SHOWS IGNEOUS ROCK ON TOP, SEDIMENTARY ROCK ON THE BOTTOM, AND METAMORPHIC ROCK IN BETWEEN.

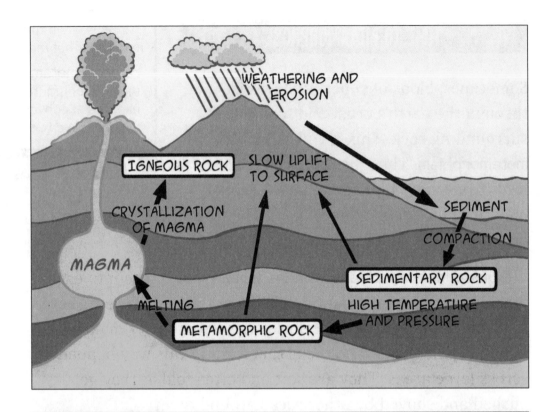

WEATHERING AND EROSION

IGNEOUS ROCK

SLOW UPLIFT TO SURFACE

CRYSTALLIZATION OF MAGMA

SEDIMENT

COMPACTION

MAGMA

SEDIMENTARY ROCK

MELTING

HIGH TEMPERATURE AND PRESSURE

METAMORPHIC ROCK

EARTH: THE ORIGINAL RECYCLER

The earth has been recycling materials for more than 4 billion years! Every rock that you see has come from another kind of rock. And every rock will eventually become another one.

Igneous rocks can erode into sediment. Sediment becomes sedimentary rocks. The sedimentary rocks can then be buried and heated and squeezed to form metamorphic rocks. Metamorphic rocks can be pushed down into the mantle and melted, to later form igneous rocks.

PS Learn about rocks from a rock song with this video!

🔍 ROCK CYCLE VIDEO CAMPUS

Why don't we see the recycling of rock in the rock cycle? It usually happens very slowly. On average, only about one half of a millimeter of rock erodes from land surfaces each year. That's about as big as the period at the end of this sentence. During millions of years, though, erosion can take down the highest mountains. The time for rock material to cycle through the mantle and rise to the crust again as magma takes hundreds of millions of years.

rock cycle: the series of events in which a rock of one type is converted to one or more other types and then back to the original type.

quartzite: a white or gray metamorphic rock that usually has no layers.

parent rock: the type of rock that another rock forms from.

WORDS ⊙ KNOW

COMMON METAMORPHIC ROCKS

Quartzite is white or gray and usually has no layers. Its parent rock—the rock type it formed from—is quartz sandstone, a sedimentary rock. Quartzite forms when quartz sandstone is placed under pressure and heats up. The "glue" holding the quartz grains together disappears and causes the grains to recrystallize. The crystals become larger and lock together.

ROCKS HAVE PARENTS, TOO

All metamorphic rocks started out as other rocks—igneous rocks, sedimentary rocks, or even other metamorphic rocks. These starting rocks are called parent rocks. You can often tell what a metamorphic rock's parent rock was, or at least narrow down the possibilities. It's like guessing the ingredients in a recipe for apple cake. You may not know exactly how much flour was used or if it contains milk, but you know that apples were one of the ingredients. It's the same way with rocks.

ROCKS AND MINERALS!

Quartzite is very hard. It often forms cliffs because it doesn't erode easily. People use quartzite for floors and stairs in buildings because it's so hard.

Marble is beautiful, and usually white or ivory colored, although it also comes in different colors. Often, these colors show up in swirling patterns. Marble's parent rock is limestone, a sedimentary rock composed of the mineral calcite. Like quartzite, marble usually has no layers. When marble forms, the grains of calcite in limestone recrystallize into larger, interlocking crystals.

··· DID YOU KNOW? ···

The Taj Mahal in Agra, India, was constructed of huge blocks of marble. Teams of up to 30 oxen moved the blocks in special carts.

Artists use marble more than any other rock for carving sculptures because it's softer than other rocks and doesn't shatter. It also glows when it's polished, so sculptures look lifelike.

A FOLDED MOUNTAIN OF QUARTZITE IN THE COUNTRY OF CHILE
CREDIT: JAMES ST. JOHN (CC BY 2.0)

slate: a type of metamorphic rock often used in construction.

schist: a type of metamorphic rock that contains a lot of mica and is not strong.

WORDS ⊚ KNOW

ROCKS FROM SHALE OR MUDSTONE

When the parent rock is shale, mudstone, or claystone, the kind of metamorphic rock that forms depends on the amount of heat or pressure. These rocks usually form from regional metamorphism in large belts. Here are a few types of these rocks.

✳ Slate forms from shale and mudstone under relatively low temperatures and pressure. Slate is dark gray, sometimes with a blue or green tint. It can also be red or brown. The grains in slate are too small to see well. Slate has been used for roofs for thousands of years because it easily breaks into flat sheets and stands up well to rain and wind.

✳ Schist has the same parent rock as slate but forms deeper underground, where temperatures and pressures are higher. Schist is usually silvery gray, brown, or yellow, and looks shiny because it contains lots of mica. The mica also gives it strong layering. The grains in schist are large enough to see without a magnifying glass. Schist isn't usually used as a building material because it isn't as strong as some other metamorphic rocks. The mica in it makes schist flake off easily.

WATCH OUT!

Fulgurite means "thunderbolt" in Latin. This metamorphic rock forms when lightning strikes sand. The extremely high temperature of the thunderbolt melts the sand grains together into glass tubes. Contact metamorphism at work!

✳ Gneiss, pronounced "nice," has shale, mudstone, or granite as its parent rock. Gneiss tends to form deep underground as the core of long mountain chains. It usually has stripes of dark gray and light-colored minerals. Gneiss is tough, so many gneiss rocks are very old. Because these rocks are beautiful and hard, they are often used for countertops and flooring.

WHY DOES EVERYONE LIKE ROCKS?

Because they're gneiss.

All the rocks we've discussed make for great collections. In the next chapter, we'll explore ways to safely identify and gather rocks to study.

? CONSIDER AND DISCUSS

It's time to consider and discuss: Why don't we notice when rocks break down and form new rocks?

WHAT ROCK IS WHERE?

Surface Sediment	Clay or Mud	Sand	Marine Animal Shells
3 miles deep, Sedimentary Rock	Shale or Mudstone	Quartz or Sandstone	Limestone
6 miles deep, Metamorphic Rock	Slate	Quartzite	Marble
9 miles deep, Metamorphic Rock	Schist	Quartzite	Marble
12 miles deep, Metamorphic Rock	Gneiss	Quartzite	Marble

SUPPLIES

* at least 3 colors of play clay
* rolling pin
* butter knife

MAKE FOLDED ROCKS

When rocks are folded, they can look different than you might expect. Try this experiment to see how folded rocks might look when you see them in the ground.

Ask an adult to help with the knife.

1 Roll out each color of clay as big and thick as a pancake. Stack the layers of clay. These are like layers of rocks.

2 With the layers flat on the table, push inward from both sides to form a fold. If the clay sticks to the table, lift the middle up into a fold.

3 Saw through one end of the folded layers with the knife. What do you notice? If a road were cut through the rocks, this is what you might see.

4 What do you think you'll see if you slice off the top at a slight angle? Try it and see. This is what happens when rocks are eroded by wind and rain.

5 Separate the colors of play clay and try the activity again, pushing the fold over on its side. Try cutting through the layers at different angles. Each time it will look a little different—just like real rocks! Sketch your observations in your science journal.

THINK ABOUT IT:

Imagine if parts of rock layers were covered by soil, and you could see just one section of folded rocks. Would you know exactly how it had folded? How might you find out?

MAKE METAMORPHIC ROCK BARS

When layered rocks are heated and turn into metamorphic rocks, their appearance can change. Try this delicious example of metamorphic rock bars and see how the ingredients look different with heat, but keep their layers.

CAUTION: Ask an adult to help with the oven!

1 Preheat the oven to 350 degrees Fahrenheit (175 degrees Celsius). Place the butter in the pan and place it in the oven for a few minutes to melt the butter. Meanwhile, wrap the graham crackers in wax paper. Pound the crackers into crumbs using the back of a spoon or your fist.

2 Remove the pan from the oven with an oven mitt. Sprinkle about 2 cups of graham cracker crumbs evenly onto the butter, covering every area.

3 Sprinkle on a layer of each of the following: chocolate chips, walnuts, other chips, and coconut flakes.

SUPPLIES

* ½ cup (1 stick) butter
* 9-by-13-inch glass baking pan
* several graham crackers
* wax paper
* oven mitts
* 12 ounces chocolate chips
* 2 cups walnut pieces
* 12 ounces butterscotch chips (or white chocolate or mint)
* 2 cups coconut flakes or raisins
* 14 ounces sweetened condensed milk

DID YOU KNOW?

Some of the buildings that have been built of marble are the Taj Mahal in India, and the Washington Monument, the Lincoln Memorial, and the Supreme Court building in Washington, DC.

HIGH-GRADE OR LOW-GRADE?

Do rocks get a grade like an A or an F? No, the "grade" of metamorphism is the amount of heat and pressure that a rock has been under. Rocks that experience greater pressure and higher temperatures change more. These rocks are called high-grade metamorphic rocks. Rocks that experience lower temperatures and pressure are called low-grade metamorphic rocks. Why do we care what grade of metamorphism a rock has experienced? Because it tells us a lot about where that rock once was. For example, some minerals form only at certain depths beneath the surface. Geologists can understand some of the history of an area from the kinds of metamorphic rocks they see. It's like putting together a puzzle.

4 Drizzle the sweetened condensed milk evenly over every area of the pan. Look through the side of the glass. Do you see layers? Make a drawing in your science journal.

5 Place in the oven and bake for about 25 minutes. Take out the pan and let cool completely. Cut into squares.

6 Look at the cut edges of your bars. Do you see layers? Did your layers stay the same or did they change? Did the color or texture or both change? Enjoy your rocks!

THINK ABOUT IT: Sometimes, in metamorphism, fluids—such as water with dissolved minerals—change rocks even more. Did you have an ingredient that acted like a fluid in a rock?

PLAY IG, SED, META!

Have you ever played rock, paper, scissors? Here's a variation to try with a friend using the rock cycle. Each player should make a fist with one hand and open the other hand flat with palm up. Tap your fist on your palm three times, saying "ig, sed, meta." After the third tap, say "go" and form one of these three shapes.

✳ An igneous rock (ig), with your fingers spread and pointing up—your fingers represent the lava and ash erupting from a volcano.

✳ A sedimentary rock (sed), with your hand facing down and parallel with the floor—this represents the flat layers of sediment that are deposited.

✳ A metamorphic rock (meta), with your thumb and fingers forming an upside-down "V"—this represents a mountain, where many metamorphic rocks are formed.

The winner of each round depends on what type of rock is formed.

If ig and sed are played, sed wins, because a sedimentary rock can form from eroded igneous rocks.

If sed and meta are played, meta wins, because metamorphic rocks can form from sedimentary rocks.

If meta and ig are played, ig wins, because when metamorphic rocks sink into the mantle, they melt to form magma, which later forms igneous rocks.

THINK ABOUT IT: If you want to get tricky, reverse things, so that ig beats sed, sed beats meta, and meta beats ig. Why do you think this way is equally correct—geologically speaking, that is?

CHAPTER 6

BECOME A ROCK HOUND!

Rocks exist all around you. Some lie nearby in their natural surroundings. Others take the form of a countertop, wall, or something else made from rock. Some people look at rocks as something to make a collection of.

Anybody can become a rock hound, including you! Even if you live in the city, you can still collect rocks. You might have already begun a collection, if you've picked up some especially pretty or interesting rocks and brought them home.

? INVESTIGATE!

How do we use rocks in our everyday life?

ROCKS AND MINERALS!

When you collect rocks, always practice safe behavior and use the rules listed here.

✳ Take an adult with you if you go outside your own backyard.

✳ Ask permission before you enter someone else's property.

✳ Collect rocks at a safe distance from the road. Stay away from rock overhangs.

✳ Never go into old mines or rock quarries because they're dangerous!

✳ Always use a rock hammer to hit rocks because a regular hammer could break and injure you.

✳ Always wear safety goggles when you hit rocks with a hammer.

✳ Wear sturdy shoes or boots and long pants.

PLACES TO FIND ROCKS

You can find rocks in two types of places. The first place is a rock outcrop, such as a cliff or place where rocks jut up from the ground. Outcrops are part of the bedrock under the soil. The second place is an area where rock fragments were deposited from somewhere else, such as streams or beaches.

Try these spots for good rock hunting.

* Your driveway, backyard, or schoolyard

* Hills and mountains

* Beaches, especially rocky seashores

* Roadsides (stay a safe distance from cars!)

* Special collecting areas (you can find these in geology guidebooks for your area)

You can also see rocks at natural history museums, rock and gem shows, or stores specializing in rocks and gems.

(PS) This website has some great resources for rock hounds. **Try the app for determining what kind of mineral you've found!**

🔍 MINEROLOGY KIDS

DID YOU KNOW?

In 1996, Christopher Wolfe, age 8, was hunting for fossils in New Mexico with his geologist father. Chris discovered a new kind of dinosaur that had horns, ate plants, and lived about 90 million years ago. The dinosaur was named after Chris, *Zuniceratops christopheri*.

Find a buddy who also wants to collect rocks and minerals. You can hunt for rocks together, and then trade them with each other or other rock-collecting friends.

When you find a rock to add to your collection, wrap it in a piece of newspaper and put a number on the newspaper. In your science journal, write down the date, where you discovered the rock, and a brief description. You might also want to take a picture or make a sketch of the rock. If you are collecting rocks from streambeds or beaches, think about where the rocks originally came from and how they reached their current location.

EQUIPMENT FOR ROCK HUNTING

You can start collecting rocks in your backyard without any special equipment. As you get more interested in rock collecting, you might want to get these other tools.

* **Rock hammer,** which is safer to use than a regular hammer because it is made from extra-strong steel.

* **Safety eye goggles,** to wear when you use a hammer to hit a rock.

* **Camera**

* **Science journal** and pencil.

* **First aid kit,** just in case.

* **Hand lens or magnifying glass,** to see crystals within rocks.

* **Sturdy backpack,** to carry rocks, equipment, food, and water.

* **Newspaper or plastic bags,** to hold your rocks.

* **Map and compass,** so you can find your way around new places.

When you get home, write the number from the newspaper on a small label and put it on the rock, so you don't lose track of what it is. You can store smaller rocks in an empty egg carton if you want.

IDENTIFYING ROCKS AND MINERALS

Don't worry if you can't tell what your rocks are yet. It can be tricky, even for experienced geologists. Here are some tips to identify rocks.

* **Where did you find your rock?** The geology of an area can tell you a lot about what kinds of rocks you might find. In the mountains, you may find granite or metamorphic rocks, such as slate. Near volcanoes, you may discover igneous rocks, such as basalt. In the Great Plains, you may find sedimentary rocks, such as limestone or sandstone.

amateur: someone who does something for enjoyment and not as a job.

WORDS TO KNOW

✴ **What minerals are in your rock?** Look very closely at it. Use a mineral identification book from the library with pictures of minerals. You can also refer to the descriptions in Chapter 2 or the link on page 26 to the Smithsonian website.

✴ **Is your rock igneous, sedimentary, or metamorphic?** If it has layers in it, it is probably either sedimentary or metamorphic. Shiny bits of mica suggest it's metamorphic, while grains of sand indicate it's sedimentary. If it's dull gray in color, earthy, or has fossils in it, it may be limestone. If the rock has crystals and no layers, it's probably igneous.

Most likely, you'll find common rocks. Check out the descriptions of common rocks in this book for help.

WHAT KIND OF DOG LOVES ROCKS?

A rock hound!

You are on your way to being an amateur geologist! By learning about the rocks that make up our world, you will be better able to understand the geological history that came before we were here. It's important to understand the history of the earth so we can make good choices in the future. So, get out there and spot some rocks!

? CONSIDER AND DISCUSS

It's time to consider and discuss: How do we use rocks in our everyday life?

PROJECT!

TREASURE HUNT

Have a treasure hunt in your house and community. Copy this list of rocks and minerals into your science journal and look for them during one week. Each time you find a rock or mineral, check it off the list and write a description of what you found and where you found it in your science journal. You will find some clues below and more clues earlier in this book.

- Fluorite (you use this every night before bed)

- Gypsum

- Salt

- Diamond

- Gold

- Apatite (you may not be able to see this, but you can feel it)

- Granite

- Marble

- Sandstone

- Limestone (you probably walk on this on the way to school)

- Graphite

- Copper (it doesn't buy as much as it used to!)

THINK ABOUT IT: How did each of these rocks or minerals get to where you found it? If a rock or mineral was part of something manmade, why do you think it was used?

acidic: from acids, which are chemical compounds that taste sour, bitter, or tart. Examples are vinegar and lemon juice. Water also contains some acid.

adapt: to make a change to better survive in the environment.

algae: a simple organism found in water that is like a plant but without roots, stems, or leaves.

amateur: someone who does something for enjoyment and not as a job.

atmosphere: the blanket of air surrounding the earth.

atom: a very small piece of matter. Atoms are the tiny building blocks of everything in the universe.

bedrock: solid rock under soil.

boundary: a line that marks a limit of an area.

carbon: the building block of most living things, including plants, as well as diamonds, charcoal, and graphite.

chemical sedimentary rock: sedimentary rock that forms when water that contains dissolved minerals evaporates and leaves behind the mineral deposits.

clast: a rock fragment such as a pebble, sand, or clay.

clastic sedimentary rock: rock that forms from rock fragments, or clasts, pressed together.

climate: the average weather in an area during a long period of time.

climate change: changes in the earth's climate patterns, including rising temperatures, which is called global warming. Climate change can happen through natural or manmade processes.

coarse-grained: rock that has mineral grains large enough to see with just your eyes.

contact metamorphism: metamorphism that happens when rocks encounter hot magma.

continental crust: the part of the earth's crust that forms the continents.

continental drift: the theory that explains how the continents have shifted on the earth's surface.

continent: one of the earth's large landmasses, including Africa, Antarctica, Australia, North America, South America, and Asia and Europe.

convergent boundary: where two tectonic plates move toward each other and come together, forming mountains and volcanoes and causing earthquakes.

core: the center of the earth, composed of the metals iron and nickel. The core has a solid inner core and a liquid outer core.

cross section: a surface or shape that is exposed by making a straight cut through something.

crust: the thin, outer layer of the earth.

crystal: a solid with atoms arranged in a geometric pattern.

dense: tightly packed.

deposit: to place.

distort: to make something look different from its normal shape.

divergent boundary: where two tectonic plates are moving in opposite directions and pulling apart, creating a rift zone. New crust forms at rift zones from the magma pushing through the crust.

durable: something that lasts for a long time.

earthquake: a sudden movement of the earth's crust caused by tectonic plates slipping along a fault.

element: a pure substance that cannot be broken down into a simpler substance. Everything in the universe is made up of combinations of elements. Oxygen, gold, and carbon are three elements.

equator: the imaginary line around the earth halfway between the North and South Poles.

erosion: the process of wearing down the earth's surface, usually by water, wind, or ice.

erupt: to burst out suddenly, such as in a volcano.

evaporate: to convert from liquid to gas.

extinction: the death of an entire species so that it no longer exists.

extrusive igneous rock: rock that forms from lava cooling and becoming solid on the surface of the earth.

fault: a crack in the earth's crust where tectonic plates move against each other.

fine-grained: rock that has mineral grains that are too small to see with just your eyes.

fossil: the remains or traces of ancient plants or animals left in rock.

gemstone: a cut or polished mineral that is beautiful, durable, and rare.

geologist: a scientist who studies geology, which is the history and structure of the earth and its rocks.

geometric: straight lines or simple shapes such as triangles or squares.

gneiss: a type of metamorphic rock often used as countertops or flooring.

greenhouse gas: a gas in the atmosphere that traps heat.

habit: the shape that the minerals in a crystal naturally tend to make.

hexagon: a shape with six sides.

Himalayas: a mountain chain between India and Tibet. It contains the world's highest mountain, Mount Everest, which is 29,029 feet above sea level.

igneous rock: rock that forms from cooling magma.

imprint: marks or indentations made by pressure.

intrusive igneous rock: rock that forms from magma cooling and becoming solid below the surface of the earth.

lava: magma that has risen to the surface of the earth.

magma: hot, partially melted rock below the surface of the earth.

mammal: a type of animal, such as a human, dog, or cat. Mammals are born live, feed milk to their young, and usually have hair or fur covering most of their skin.

mantle: the middle layer of the earth between the crust and the core.

marble: a type of metamorphic rock often used for sculptures.

metamorphic rock: rock that was transformed by heat or pressure or both into new rocks, while staying solid.

metamorphosis: the process some animals go through in their life cycle. They change size, shape, and color.

meteorite: a meteoroid that is not burned up by the earth's atmosphere, so it hits the earth's surface. A meteoroid is a rock that orbits the sun. It is smaller than an asteroid and at least as large as a speck of dust.

Mid-Atlantic Ridge: a plate boundary on the floor of the Atlantic Ocean, and part of the longest mountain range in the world.

mineral: a naturally occurring solid found in rocks and in the ground. Rocks are made of minerals. Gold and diamonds are precious minerals.

molten: made liquid by heat.

nucleus: the central part of the cell that controls how it functions.

oceanic crust: the earth's crust under the oceans.

organic sedimentary rock: rock that forms from the remains of plants and animals.

organic: something that is or was living.

organism: a living thing, such as a plant or animal.

outcrop: a rock formation that is visible on the surface.

oxygen: the most abundant element on the earth, found in air, water, and many rocks.

paleontology: the study of the history of life on Earth through the study of the fossils of plants and animals.

parent rock: the type of rock that another rock forms from.

plate tectonics: the theory that describes how tectonic plates in the earth's crust move slowly and interact with each other to produce earthquakes, volcanoes, and mountains.

pore: a tiny opening.

pressure: a continuous force that pushes on an object.

quartzite: a white or gray metamorphic rock that usually has no layers.

rare: something there is not very many or much of.

recycle: to use something again.

regional metamorphism: metamorphism that happens at convergent tectonic plate boundaries.

rift: an area where the earth's crust is being pulled apart.

rock: a solid, natural substance made up of minerals.

rock cycle: the series of events in which a rock of one type is converted to one or more other types and then back to the original type.

rock hound: a person who collects rocks and minerals for a hobby.

schist: a type of metamorphic rock that contains a lot of mica and is not strong.

sediment: small particles of rocks or minerals, such as clay, sand, or pebbles.

sedimentary rock: rock formed from sediment, the remains of plants or animals, or the evaporation of seawater.

seismic wave: the wave of energy that travels outward from an earthquake.

silicon: an abundant element found in sand, clay, and quartz.

slate: a type of metamorphic rock often used in construction.

solution: one substance dissolved into another.

stalactite: a cave formation that looks like an icicle hanging from the ceiling.

stalagmite: a cave formation projecting up from the floor, often underneath a stalactite.

tectonic plates: large sections of the earth's crust that move on top of the hot, melted layer below.

theory: an unproven idea that tries to explain why something is the way it is.

transform boundary: where two tectonic plates slide against each other.

universe: everything that exists, everywhere.

volcano: an opening in the earth's surface through which lava, ash, and gases can burst out.

volume: the amount of space occupied by something.

METRIC CONVERSIONS

Use this chart to find the metric equivalents to the English measurements in this book. If you need to know a half measurement, divide by two. If you need to know twice the measurement, multiply by two. How do you find a quarter measurement? How do you find three times the measurement?

English	Metric
1 inch	2.5 centimeters
1 foot	30.5 centimeters
1 yard	0.9 meter
1 mile	1.6 kilometers
1 pound	0.5 kilogram
1 teaspoon	5 milliliters
1 tablespoon	15 milliliters
1 cup	237 milliliters

BOOKS

Chin, Jason. *Grand Canyon*. Roaring Brook Press, 2017.

DK Publishing. *The Rock and Gem Book: And Other Treasures of the Natural World*. DK Children, 2016.

Guillain, Charlotte. *The Street Beneath My Feet*. words & pictures, 2017.

Reilly, Kathleen M. *Fault Lines & Tectonic Plates: Discover What Happens When the Earth's Crust Moves With 25 Projects*. Nomad Press, 2017.

Smith, Miranda and Sean Callery. *Rocks, Minerals & Gems*. Scholastic Nonfiction, 2016.

MUSEUMS AND SCIENCE CENTERS

The Academy of Natural Sciences of Drexel University, Philadelphia, Pennsylvania
ansp.org

The Burke Museum of Natural History and Culture, Seattle, Washington
burkemuseum.org

Carnegie Museum of Natural History, Pittsburgh, Pennsylvania
carnegiemnh.org

The Field Museum, Chicago, Illinois
fieldmuseum.org

The Mineral Museum of Michigan, Houghton, Michigan
museum.mtu.edu

Mineralogical Museum at Harvard University, Cambridge, Massachusetts
mgmh.fas.harvard.edu

Smithsonian National Museum of Natural History, Washington, DC
mnh.si.edu/earth

Yale University Peabody Museum of Natural History, New Haven, Connecticut
peabody.yale.edu

University of California Museum of Paleontology, Berkeley, California
ucmp.berkeley.edu

WEBSITES

Extreme Science: extremescience.com

National Park Service: nps.gov

Science News for Kids: sciencenewsforkids.org

The Story of the Haddonfield "Bone Wars"
levins.com/dinosaur

The Story of the Hope Diamond at the Smithsonian
naturalhistory2.si.edu/mineralsciences/hope

Strange Science – The Rocky Road to Modern Paleontology and Biology
strangescience.net

U.S. Geological Survey (U.S.G.S.): usgs.gov

U.S.G.S. Earthquakes for Kids
earthquake.usgs.gov/learn/kids

U.S.G.S. in your schoolyard
usgs.gov/science-support/osqi/yes/resources-teachers/school-yard-geology

ESSENTIAL QUESTIONS

Introduction: Where can you find some rocks and minerals to study?

Chapter 1: How does movement on the surface and deep inside the earth create new rocks?

Chapter 2: What makes one type of mineral different from another?

Chapter 3: How do igneous rocks form?

Chapter 4: Why do sedimentary rocks usually have layers?

Chapter 5: Why don't we notice when rocks break down and form new rocks?

Chapter 6: How do we use rocks in our everyday life?

QR CODE GLOSSARY

Page 7: youtube.com/watch?v=WCeSP8bqY1w

Page 16: youtube.com/watch?v=RgJZ0ySEKYg

Page 17: google.com/earth

Page 26: geogallery.si.edu/gems

Page 38: youtube.com/watch?v=1FEvv8hgkO4

Page 53: youtube.com/watch?v=IkN0olZ51OM

Page 68: youtube.com/watch?v=G7xFfezsJ1s

Page 79: mineralogy4kids.org